PART ONE

Greetings and Manners

Don Corleone, I am honoured and grateful that you have invited me to your daugh . . . ter 's wedding . . . on the day of your daughter's wedding. And I hope their first child be a masculine child. I pledge my ever-ending loyalty.

Luca Brasi, *The Godfather*

Whether you are planning to receive fawning supplicants from the local community, welcoming other *capi* (bosses) to your daughter's wedding or simply paying a relaxed, friendly visit to a restaurant or bar with ten heavily armed henchmen, a 'made man' must always show – and more importantly, be given – respect (*rispetto*).

Greeting an ordinary member of the public, family (as opposed to Family) members and 'friends of yours'* couldn't be easier. Simply smile, pretend to smile or curl your lip with disgust – you're the one in charge, after all – and say...

* Not to be confused with 'friends of *ours*' – see glossary.

Hi!

Ciao!
[TchOW!]

How are you?

Come stai?
[Commay-STY?]

My compliments on your beautiful restaurant*

Complimenti! Hai un ristorante bellissimo.
[Com-plee-MEN-tee! Hi oon riss-tor-AN-tay
bel-EE-simo]

*"I would hate to see it accidentally burnt to the ground." *Mi dispiacerebbe tanto,
vederlo distrutto dal fuoco.* [Me diss-pee-ah-cher-EB-bay tanto, ved-AIR-lo
dist-ROOT-oh dal fwO-cko]

Greeting another 'made man'
(un' uomo combinato)

As every Mafioso knows, it is considered very bad form, when meeting another member of the Family, to introduce oneself directly as a fellow 'man of honour' (*uomo d'onore*). If at all possible, a third 'made' friend should make the connection clear by presenting person A to person B in appropriately vague terms such as 'He is a friend of ours' or 'You two are the same thing as me'.

If a third *uomo combinato* is not around, you might like to instead use a traditional method employed by the Sicilian Mafia for spotting a fellow Family member: a cryptic conversation about 'toothache' that acts rather like a Masonic handshake. In 1875, the Chief of Police of Palermo obtained a transcript of one such introductory conversation – which goes on to reveal details of the Mafia's secret initiation ceremony – for the Italian Minister of the Interior. Using a variation on the Chief of Police's transcript as a loose template, here is a fun roleplay that you might like to try with a friend, replacing the names and places with your own personal details:

Roleplay!

A: (*Pointing to one of your front teeth*) *Mannaggia*!* I have a terrible toothache.

B: Me too.

A: Tell me, friend. How did you come by this affliction?

B: I met with friends of ours in the town of Corleone, on the day of Our Lady of the Annunciation.

A: Who were these friends?

B: Beppe Lollobrigida and Giuseppe Gotti.

A: I know them well. Fine, upstanding men, both of whom also have terrible trouble with their teeth.

B: You speak the truth.

A: And what happened at this meeting, friend?

B: Beppe Lollobrigida lit a candle and took me to one side. He cut open my hand with a sharp blade, took the holy image of a saint, smeared it with my blood and burned the icon. He scattered the ashes to the four winds, which is the fate of all traitors.

A: Great. Er, so did you see the game last night?

You may now continue the conversation at your leisure, safe in the knowledge that your new friend is 'the same thing as you'.

*Dammit!

Nice to meet you!

Piacere!
[Pee-atch-AIR-ay!]

TRAVEL TIP

THE 'DON'

Sicily is a vibrant melting pot of cultures, an island of sunshine, lemon trees and deep blue sea that has been occupied, over the centuries, by Greece, Rome, Spain, France and even Britain. The title of 'Don', and the custom of kissing the hand as a mark of respect, harks back to the long period of Spanish rule, when high-ranking members of the ruling foreign nobility were afforded lavish respect by their feudal underlings.

Such gestures outlived the Spanish occupation, and came to be offered to any man of standing in Sicilian society, whether the 'Don' in question was *un uomo combinato* or not. If you are to be afforded proper respect when meeting new people in your own home or in a local bar or restaurant, rest assured that you are therefore well within your rights to offer your hand disdainfully to the landlord for him to kiss it, and to introduce yourself using the term 'Don' before your surname (e.g. Don Perignon, Don Brown, Don Osmond).

USEFUL CLICHÉS!

Now that you are ready to meet and greet fellow hoodlums in your area with confidence, why not try sprinkling these gangster film clichés into conversations with your new-found friends?

I think we're going to get on just fine
Credo che andremo tutti d'accordo
[Cray-doe kay an-drem-oh TOOT-ie dak-OR-doh]

My house is your house
La mia casa è la tua casa
[La me-a ka-za eh la TU-a ka-za]

You are like a brother to me
Per me sei come un fratello
[Pear MAY say commay oon frat-ELL-oh]

If you ever need anything, I want you to come ask me, okay?
Se hai bisogna di qualcosa, devi chiedermi un favore, va bene?
[Say hi biz-ON-ya dee kwal-koza, dev-ee kee-ED-air-me oon fav-OR-ay, va BEN-ay?]

PART TWO

Common Expressions

Somebody messes with me,

I'm gonna mess with him.

Al Capone, *The Untouchables*

In order to be taken seriously in your new *mandamento* (district), you will need to know when to wax lyrical, when to resort to gangster clichés, and when to show an appropriate level of disdain towards underlings and local businesses. Included in this section of the phrasebook you will find lots of useful lines with which to spice up everyday 'conversations'*, but let's start with the important part first: as a wannabe Mafioso, you have to know when to shut up . . .

Careless talk costs lives!

Some say that *Omertà* – the famous Mafia code of silence – comes from the Italian word for 'humility', *umiltà* ('*umirta*' in Sicilian dialect). Other etymologists point to the Latin for 'man', *homo*, as a possible root, making the word a powerful symbol of 'manliness'. As shown in the three Sicilian gestures opposite, however, the important point is not the word's history, but its meaning to the Family: 'Hear nothing, see nothing, say nothing; leave us to get on with our business, or face the consequences.' Or, to put it more succinctly: 'You ain't seen nuthin', right?'

*beatings

1. Hear nothing

Non sentire
[Non sent-EER-ay]

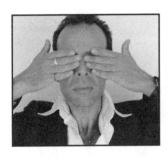

2. See nothing

Non vedere
[Non ved-AIR-ay]

3. Say nothing

Non parlare
[Non pah-LAR-ay]

Mum's the word

Acqua in bocca*
[A-kwa in BOK-ka]

*Literally, 'water in mouth' – so full of water, that is, that you are unable to speak and let the secret slip out... The gesture can be anything signifying a closure of the mouth, a zipping or locking motion being common variations.

THE FIFTH AMENDMENT:
REMAINING POLITE UNDER QUESTIONING

When Frank 'Lefty' Rosenthal (the real-life study for Robert de Niro's character in the film *Casino*) testified in a 1961 Congressional Hearing on gambling, he is said to have exercised his Fifth Amendment privilege against self-incrimination no fewer than thirty-seven times. Using Rosenthal's textbook answer under fire, why not try these simple exchanges with a friend. To inject some realism into proceedings, your fellow role player may like to knock you around a bit, to see if you are able to maintain grace under pressure:

Roleplay!

A: Is your name Colin 'the dumptruck' Spiggot, of 27 Acacia Avenue, London?

B: I respectfully decline to answer the question, as I honestly believe my answer might tend to incriminate me.

A: Are you right-handed?

B: I respectfully decline to answer the question, as I honestly believe my answer might tend to incriminate me.

A: So that's one 9-inch Hawaiian with coleslaw, diet cola and a balloon on a stick for the child. Would you like the crust deep pan, traditional or stuffed?

B: I respectfully decline to answer that question, as I honestly believe... Sorry, I mean, deep pan, thanks. With extra mushrooms, *capiche*?

What do you want?

Che vuoi?*
[Kay-VOY?]

*Rather than being used to illustrate a polite request for information, the
connotation of this gesture is more one of exasperation or impatience. It can
be performed with one hand held out in front or with two hands, as shown,
the hands being shaken with varying degrees of violence, depending on the
extent to which your companion is 'breaking your balls'.

Don't worry about it

Non ti preoccupare
[Non tee pray-ok-oo-PAR-ay]

Now hold on a minute...

Aspetta un attimo
[Ass-PET-ah oon ATT-imo]

Everyday Tasks

As a made man, you will find that many everyday dealings with salespersons and merchants are more complex than before, and that you want more from their products than you did previously. Here is an example of a conversation you might find yourself in. Note the amiable, respectful tone 'our friend' keeps in the face of the shopkeeper's rank insolence:

BUYING FISHING LINE

Mafioso: How strong is this line? It take plenty of strain?

Shopkeeper: That, sir, is our superior fishing line. It can take as much strain as any fish can put on it.

M: I'm not convinced. Say I catch, like, a two-hundred-forty pound fish, would this finish him off?

S: With all respect, I'm not sure there is such a fish to be caught in the state of New Jersey, sir.

M: Trust me. Say we land this big fish, he's still not dead and I'm with my friends – some of whom are very ignorant about fishing methods – and they decide to throttle him with it?

S: Then, sir, I should say you might want to try our extra-strength reinforced line, which is just over here . . .

What you say is of no interest to me.

Non me ne importa niente*
[Non may nay im-por-ta nee-EN-tay]

*Feel free to inject as much disgust as you like while touching your fingertips to the underside of your chin, and sweeping forwards in one gloriously dismissive motion.

So I like violins. What of it?

Mi piaciono i violini. E allora?
[Me pee-atch-ono ee veeo-LEE-nee. Eh a LOR-a?]

What a bore*

Che peso
[Kay PEZ-oh]

*Literally 'what a weight'. The metaphorical meaning extends to anything that is a burden to the speaker, e.g. 'This crackdown by the *poliziotti* is really ruining business'.

'Bollocks'

Due palle cosi*
[Do-ay pal-ay ko-ZEE]

*Literally: 'Two balls, right here', to indicate just how impressed you are with a particularly tiresome individual or situation.

USEFUL CLICHÉS!

I swear on all the saints/on my mother's grave
Lo giuro su tutti i santi e sulla tomba di mia madre
[Low joor-oh sue toot-ee ee sant-ee eh sulla tom-ba dee
me-a MA-dray]

I'm afraid the gentleman you're asking for don't live round
here no more
Mi dispiace ma il tizio che cerca non abita più qui
[Me dis-pee-ATCH-ay ma eel titz-ee-oh kay cherka non
abita pyu kwee]

There's something going on here . . . and I don't like it
C'è qualcosa che mi puzza . . .
[Chay kwal-koza kay me POOTZ-a . . .]

I knew, from the first moment I saw you, that you were a
man of honour, a man of respect
*L'ho capito subito che eri un uomo d'onore, un uomo di
rispetto.*
[Low kap-EE-to SOO-bit-oh kay air-ee oon wommo don-
OR-ay, oon wommo dee ris-PET-to]

He was a good man.

Era un buon tipo
[AIR-a oon bwon TEE-po]

PART THREE

Business

'I'll make him an offer
he can't refuse.'

Michael Corleone, *The Godfather*

An accomplished Mafia Don will take the time to master many traditional skills in order to make an honest living, from racketeering to protection, drug dealing, arms trading, pornography, robbery and money laundering. Some even stoop to politics.

You can master every outward sign of being a Mafioso, have the look, the clothes and the gestures just right, but it is in your working life as a businessman that you will truly earn your spurs. No stuffy open-plan 'pods' for you; your office is the great city itself, from the dimly lit lower levels of multistorey car parks to lonely subways, frozen meat lockers and the back rooms of local restaurants. Study our guide to Mafia business and rest assured that if enough of your enemies end up sleeping with the fishes, the world will be your oyster.

'Something is going on between those two'/'Those two are meeting in private'

Questi due se la intendono
[KWEST-ee DO-ay say la inTEND-ono]
Sicilian: Sti dui filìanu.

Money/Bread

Soldi/Grana*
[SOLD-ee/GRAH-na]

*A gesture to be used instead of having to say out loud that it's time for the protection money, or *pizzo*, to be paid.

Contentment/Happiness

Contentezza*
[Con-ten-TETZ-a]

*Perhaps after having closed a deal for a great quantity of cheesecake, with extra cream. See pp44/45, 'Doing business over the phone'.

I swear it.*

Lo giuro
[Low DJOO-ro]

*The front, back and front of the index and second fingers are kissed quickly, turning the hand in quick succession.

'He's a bad sort/not to be trusted' or, paradoxically, 'He's cool/ok'

'Facciataglia'*
[FATCH-eea-TAL-ya]

*literally 'cut-face'.

The deal stinks

Che puzza*
[Kay POOTZ-a]

*Literally: 'what an awful smell'.

'Bottled-up anger'

'Collera interna'
[Koll-air-a in-TER-na]

He's in prison

È detenuto
[Ay detten-OO-toe]

It's stuck in my throat.*

Mi è rimasto in gola.
[Me ay ree-MAS-toe in GO-la]

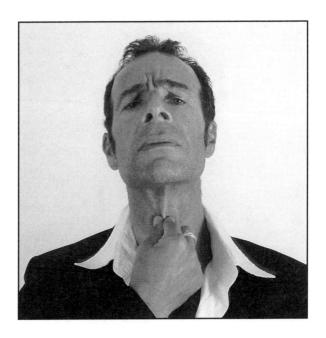

*This gesture indicates that, metaphorically speaking, you find it hard to digest a
piece of news, a missed opportunity or an uncomfortable situation. E.g. 'I am
displeased by the news that my daughter wishes to marry Sergeant O'Hoolihan.'

He's a cop/a grass!

Sbirro! / 'Cascittuni'*
[SBEE-roh / Cashi-TOO-ni]

*A 'cascittuni', in Palermo dialect, is the toilet of a prison cell. Anyone found to have informed to the authorities is said to have had their head dunked in the cascittuni; metaphorically, the smell of such a person never goes away . . .

No good/I don't have any/I can't do it.

Niente!
[Nee-ENT-ay]

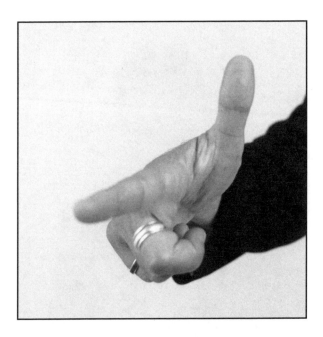

*Point with the thumb extended at right angles as shown, and holding the position rigidly, rotate the wrist left and right, moving the thumb but keeping the extended finger more or less still.

Help me, Godfather! I beg you!

Aiutami padrino! La prego!
[Eye-OO-tamee pad-ree-no! La PRAY-go!]

And am I just supposed to stand here like a jamook?

E io che sto, a guardare?
[Ay EE-oh kay stow, ah gwa-DAH-ray?]
Sicilian: E io chi fazzu, lu pupu?

*The hand is held in the position shown and rotated three or four times from the wrist while speaking.

I know nothing/I wash my hands of this business

Non so niente
[Non so nee-ENT-ay]

Word of honour.

Parola d'onore
[Pa-roll-ah don-OR-ay]

Doing business over the phone

Fellow made men: be careful! As a new mafioso, you will find that many of your business practices, while both profitable and undoubtedly providing a service to society, are frowned upon by certain government-sponsored organizations. The FBI are everywhere, and they are recording your conversations. You would be well advised therefore to substitute any key words for pre-agreed codewords, as in the famous FBI transcript of an alleged drug deal involving original 'wiseguy' Henry Hill, in which two men discuss the furtive exchange of golf clubs, dog pills and a great deal of top quality, uncut shampoo. Read out the following fictional roleplay with a friend, imagining all the time that the Feds are listening . . .

Roleplay!

Mafioso 1: You get the golf clubs?

Mafioso 2: Yeah, but I didn't get no ice cream.

M1: No ice cream? What, was it too expensive?

M2: No, he says he don't sell ice cream no more. He got cheesecake up to the eyeballs but no ice cream. The golf clubs is stashed.

M1: What kind of cheesecake, the kind we used in Las Vegas that time?

M2: No, bigger cheesecake. Like the type our friend went on vacation because of.

M1: God rest his soul. Okay, get the golf clubs to our friend with the two dogs, and I want as much cheesecake as he'll sell us. And cream, like to go on the cheesecake? We'll need as much cream as possible.

M2: He got that too, Boss. We're gonna have ourselves quite a tea party.

USEFUL CLICHÉS!

How can you ask me such a thing? You break my heart
Come puoi chiedermi una cosa del genere? Mi spezzi il cuore
[Kommay poy kee-ED-air-me oona koza del jen-er-ay? Me
spetzee eel kWOR-ay]

Never ask me about business
Non chiedermi mai dei miei affari
[Non kee-ed-air-me MY day-ee me-ay-ee af-FAR-ee]

I'm going to be taking care of things around here from
now on . . .
Da ora in poi me ne occupo io . . .
[Da or-a in poy may nay ok-oo-po EE-oh]

I don't trust nobody
Non mi fido di nessuno
[Non me feed-oh dee ness-OO-no]

I've paid my debt to society!
Ho pagato il mio debito verso la società!
[Oh pag-a-toe eel me-o DEB-it-oh vair-so la sotch-ee-et-A]

PART FOUR

Insults and Threats

'BadaBING!'

Sonny Corleone, *The Godfather*

According to at least one respected Italian Mafia expert*, behaving '*in maniera mafiosa*' ('like a Mafioso') resides above all in the need to command respect ('*farsi rispettare*'). You will notice that more often than not, such respect is given freely by the local community; after all, in return for a very reasonable monthly *pizzo*, you provide them with peace of mind and protection against their shop windows being smashed, their close relatives being garrotted and fed to the pigs and all manner of similar household accidents and acts of God.

Sometimes, however, even your kindly patronage will not be enough to persuade people to donate their hard-earned money to keep you in the manner to which you have become accustomed. The severed heads of million-dollar racehorses not being available at many supermarkets, you may therefore find the following insults and threats useful when visiting local businesses and in your dealings with bent cops or underlings.

*Pino Arlacchi, *La Mafia imprenditrice* (Bologna, Il Mulino, 1983)

You're crazy!

Sei pazzo/Sei fuori*
[Say PATZ-oh/Say FWOR-ee]

*Holding your hand up next to your temple, fan the fingers of your hand quickly as seen in the photograph, accompanied by a snappy flick of the wrist (little finger first, then fourth finger, then middle etc.). The movement carries with it a sense of empty space.

Nothing*

Niente/nulla.
[Nee-EN-tay/NULL-a]

*If you can muster an appropriate level of disdain in your expression, this comes to mean, by extension: 'You are worth nothing to me.'

'Horns'*

Corna
[KOR-na]

*Pointing downwards, a gesture used to ward off bad luck (a 'scongiuro'), or as a curse.

'Cuckold'*

Cornuto
[Kor-NOO-toe]
Sicilian: Curnutu

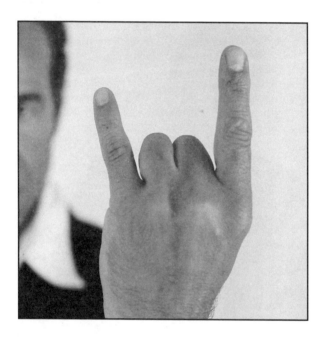

*Used as an insult, but in certain circumstances it can also mean 'shrewd',
or 'cunning'.

Up yours!

Vafanculo!
[Va-fan-COOL-oh!]

Funny how? I amuse you?

Come buffo? Ti faccio ridere?
[COM-may BOOF-oh? Tee fatch-oh REE-der-ay?]

Fuggedaboudit.

Dimenticalo
[Dee-MEN-ti-callo]

Fuggedaboudit.

Dimenticalo
[Dee-MEN-ti-callo]

Fuggedaboudit.

Dimenticalo
[Dee-MEN-ti-callo]

I'll smash your face in!

Ti spacco la faccia!
[Tea spak-oh la FATCH-ee-a]

Keep your mouth shut!

Stai zitto!
[Sty tzEE-toe]

You will pay dearly.*

Ti faccio un culo cosi!
[Tee fatch-oh oon coo-loh koh-ZEE]

* (Literally: 'I'll tear you a new arsehole this big'.) This gesture can also be used to mean that someone has 'arse', meaning 'luck'; or that someone has worked very hard (so hard as to tear *themselves* a new arsehole this big . . .)

I'm watching you

Ti tengo d'occhio
[Tea ten-go DOK-yo]

I'll give you such a slap!

Ti do uno schiaffo
[Tee doe oono skee-AFF-oh]

Damn you!/If I get hold of you . . .*

Mannaggia a te!/Se t'acchiappo . . .
[Man-NAH-jah ah tay! Say tak-YAP-oh]

*[. . . I'll bite you like THIS!]

Dead.*

Morto
[MORE-toe]
Sicilian: 'ntustò

* As in: 'I'm afraid our friend doesn't live here no more.' The index– and second fingers are held together and circled upwards two or three times in a small, quick motion, as in a 'regal' wave.

Threat

Minaccia*
[Min-ATCH-ee-a]

*A threatening gesture that slashes across the throat sharply.

'Spring cleaning'

As a mob underboss or *capodecina*, you will be in charge of at least ten *picciotti* or *soldati* ('foot soldiers'). (*Capodecina* literally means 'head of ten'). It is a depressing fact that sooner or later, the loyalty of these men will be called into question, whether by a rival outfit or a Federal Grand Jury. At this point it is essential you know how to discipline your underlings in order to retain their respect. If a *soldato* is suspected of acting out of line, there are two ways in which to deal with him:

1. IF YOU SUSPECT HE IS INNOCENT

An ideal location for this encounter would be a disused warehouse, municipal swimming pool or the empty pitch of a local football stadium at night. To prevent his attention from wandering, tie your *soldato* to a chair, and get various 'young Turks' to surround him in a circle. Baseball bats and other robustly made sporting equipment may come in useful, and should be kept within easy reach.

> **Capo:** Carlo, I never expected this from you.
>
> **Soldato:** I never spoke to Sergeant O'Hoolihan! It's not true! I hate that man with all my soul! You know my only loyalty is to you!
>
> **Capo:** But we got witnesses putting you in McClusky's Ice Cream Parlour with him Tuesday morning.

Soldato:	What witnesses? They're lying! I swear on my mother's grave, I never spoke to him!
Capo:	(*Sighing heavily*) If only your poor mother could see you now, Carlo. She was a good woman. She never brought you up to be a rat. Boys, I think Carlo needs a little more . . . *encouragement* . . .

Such dialogue can be repeated, with minor variations, as many times as you wish, until either a) you become tired, or b) the innocent *soldato* passes out, or expires (see p25 for the appropriate response to this unexpected tragedy). Note a swift increase of respect towards yourself from your men and a general rise in the crew's morale.

2. IF YOU SUSPECT HE IS GUILTY

The only truly effective location for this encounter is your own home. Make an occasion of it: throw a party, post guards at the gates, break out the best champagne and food. After a gigantic midday feast, pull the guilty *soldato* to one side for a chat. Ensure that other trusted wiseguys are gathered nearby, looking friendly and concerned.

Capo:	Carlo, I'm worried about you, you been looking stressed.
Soldato:	Me stressed? No, boss, I'm feeling better than ever.

Capo:	Even now you sweat as I talk to you. This is stressful work, Carlo, and don't let nobody say I don't reward all my men. You're gonna go on holiday. Bright lights, big city. I got it all booked for you. Here are the tickets.
Soldato:	(*Looking pale*) Gee, that's very kind of you boss.
Capo:	(*With expansive, magnanimous gestures to the gallery*) I never trusted nobody like I trusted you, Carlo. You're like a brother to me. We always looked out for each other when we were kids and I want to make sure you're okay. Here, have some money too.
Soldato:	(*Weakly*) You always been very good to me, boss.
Capo:	(*Fondly*) Look at this suit, it's falling apart, you do me disrespect wearing this. Get a new one. Cut your hair, sit by the pool, get yourself a woman for the week. You're gonna feel like a new man . . .

Allow him to be led to the car, where an enforcer will be waiting in the back seat with all the equipment necessary to make it anatomically difficult for the errant *soldato* to betray you again. Note a swift increase of respect towards yourself from your men and a general etc . . .

USEFUL CLICHÉS!

I want him to meet with a little . . . accident
Potrebbe capitargli un piccolo . . . incidente
[Pot-rebb-ay kapit-AR-lee oon pik-ollo . . . in-chee-DENT-ay]

I want you to go on a short ride with the boys
Vorrei che tu facessi un giretto in macchina con i picciotti
[Vorray kay to fatch-ess-ee oon ji-RET-oh in mak-ina con ee
    pitch-YOTT-ee]

We got our laws. You broke our laws
Noi abbiamo le nostre leggi. Tu le hai infrante.
[Noy ab-yamo lay nos-tray ledge-ee. To lay hi in-FRANT-ay]

You come here to *my house* and you talk about corrup-
    tion/murder/dishonour (etc.)
*Tu hai il coraggio di venire a casa mia, a parlarmi di cor-
    ruzione/crimini/disonore . . .*
[To hi eel kor-adgio dee ven-ee-ray a kaza ME-ya, a par-lar-
    me dee korrootz-ee-OH-nay/KRIM-i-nee/diz-ON-or-ay . . .]

PART FIVE

Food and Drink

'How much money did you give that guy? A wiseguy never pays for his drinks.'

Lefty, *Donnie Brasco*

Finally, a chance to relax. After a hard day of beating *pentiti*, extorting money and aiming heavy machine guns out of the windows of speeding cars, your limbs are tired and you deserve a good meal. Fortunately you will find that, as a result of your high social standing, there is such a thing as a free lunch. Many of the finest eateries in town will fall over themselves to provide you and your friends with sustenance, but in order to be taken seriously, you will first need to know a few pointers and gestures...

Fancy a coffee?

Prendiamo un caffè?*
(Pren-dee-AH-mo oon kaffAY?)

* Remember to extend the little finger, and make a sharp, snappy tipping motion, as if downing a tiny shot of industrial strength *espresso*.

Let's have a drink!

Beviamo qualcosa?*
[Bev-ee-AH-mo kwal-KO-za?]

*Although any Mafioso worth his salt will want something a good deal stronger, many readers may wish to know that a cold beer can be suggested thus: 'Prendiamo una birra?' [Pren-dee-AH-mo oona BE-ra?]

Cheers!

Salute!
[Sal-OOT-ay!]

Going into the restaurant business is a very common sideline for Mafiosi, and you will find it to be a most enjoyable addition to the Family's portfolio. Business negotiations will roughly follow these three stages:

Roleplay!

STAGE 1

Restaurateur: Good evening, sir. Welcome to *Fabrizzio's*.

Mafioso: Good evening. I would like to sit at your best table.

R: Of course. Come this way.

M: I'm afraid I find myself without my wallet. I take it this will not prevent you serving me or my fourteeen friends.

R: Of course not. Lobster and champagne for these customers!

STAGE 2

Mafioso: You see I enjoyed my last meal here as I have returned. I trust our boisterousness did not alarm you.

Restaurateur: It was most highly entertaining! My stitches will be removed tomorrow and the grand piano was always a vulgar addition. I am pleased to be rid of it. Roberto, a table for twenty six!

M: Now that we are such good friends, I feel I may ask you a favour. I am embarrassed by a temporary cash-flow problem and may need to borrow some money.

R: Roberto has already emptied the till into a paper bag and placed it in your coat pocket. Also, I offer my daughter's company that she might entertain you.

Daughter: Father, no!

R: Be quiet.

M: You are indeed a friend.

STAGE 3:

R: I see my favourite customer has returned.

M: I come with a heavy heart. I see no other customers here and since our acquaintance your business seems to be failing.

R: You are quite right. All of a sudden, and entirely due to my own mismanagement, we find ourselves without any stock or money and with our windows smashed.

M: As a favour to you my associates have poured petrol over the establishment to assist you in claiming the insurance. Take these matches. Also, I am grieved for your loss.

R: She was a very wilful girl.

Excellent.

Eccelente!
[Etch-a-LENT-ay]

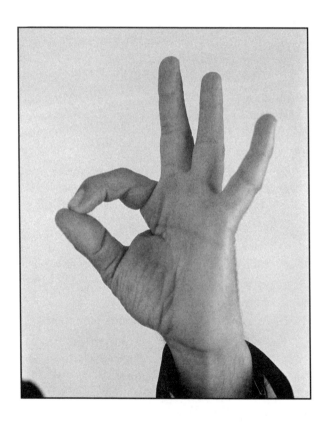

Just a bit more

Un pochino di più
[Ooh pok-EE-no dee PYOU]

Delicious!

Squisito!
[Skw-EEZ-it-oh]

I have eaten well.

Ho mangiato bene.*
[Oh man-gee-AH-toe ben-ay]

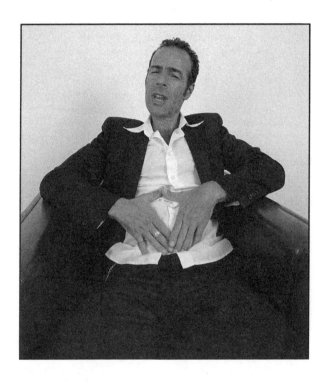

*[Editor's note: You will definitely need to learn this gesture.]

The bill, please!

Il conto, per favore!*
[Eel CON-toe, pear fav-OR-ay!]

*[Editor's note: You will never need to learn this gesture.]

Glossary

Administration	The powerful upper levels of the Family's hierarchy, comprising the *capo*, underboss and *consigliere*
Associate:	Somebody who is not yet a made man, but who nonetheless works for the family and may yet be invited to take the vow of silence
The books are open	In a world where nothing is said, and nothing is written down, this phrase has become an ironic byword for 'membership'. If there is a position available within the organization, then 'the books are open'. When 'the books are closed', do not be expected to receive an invitation to burn the image of a saint
Boss, Don, Chairman	The head of the organization; the man who decides how much cheesecake to buy, who gets made, and who is to meet with a little accident
Babania	Heroin. (a.k.a shampoo, dog pills, golf clubs, cheesecake . . .)
Babbo	A dummy/idiot/useless underling
Borgata, brugad	An organized crime Family
Broken	Demoted; stripped of power within the organization
Buttlegging	Bootlegging untaxed cigarettes
Button	A goodfella/*uomo d'onore*
Cafone, 'Gavone'	Literally, a 'peasant' – an embarrassment to the Family
Capice? (American slang for the Italian *capisci*?)	Understand?
Captain, Skipper, *Capocosca*	Ranking family member who leads a small body of men
Capo di tutti capi	The man seen by the authorities and press, if not by the Families themselves, as the 'Boss of Bosses'. Traditionally, the title went to the *capo* of the most poweful of the five Families of New York, who there- fore had the role of Chairman at inter-Family Commission meetings
Cazzia, stugots	From *stu cazzo or u'cazzu*, the testicles
Chased	To be cast out from the Mafia – a merciful punishment, since the alternative may involve very heavy shoes, and a very deep body of water

Cleaning	The careful avoidance of being followed, while in a car
Clip, whack, hit, pop, burn, put a contract out, break an egg, do a piece of work, ice	Murder
Comare	The mistress of a Mafioso
Combinato	'Made'; initiated into the Mafia
The Commision (*Commissione*)	The Mafia's Supreme council, typically a meeting of the bosses of the five New York Families: Gambino, Genovese, Lucchese, Colombo and Bonanno, though Families controlling other powerful areas such as the city of Chicago were often invited to send delegates
Compare	Sidekick, crony, close friend. Literally, 'godfather' (in the standard sense) in Italian
Confirm	To be made
Consigliere	Robert Duvall in *The Godfather*. The 'chief whip' of the Family; a man whose wisdom and cunning is highly valued by the Boss
Cosca (plural: *cosche*)	Sicilian dialect word for 'artichoke', which has come to mean 'a Mafia family'. Metaphorically, Mafiosi cling together tightly, like the leaves of an artichoke
Crank	Speed
Crew	The small group of *soldati* led by a capo
Cugine	A young Turk well on the way to being 'made' (literally 'cousin' in Italian)
CW	Co-operating Witness: FBI term
Eat alone	To be greedy, keep a piece of the action to oneself
Empty suit	Someone with little to offer the Mafia, but who tags along nonetheless
Enforcer	The classic Mafia tough guy; Luca Brasi in *The Godfather*
Family	An organized crime association
Friend of mine	Used by a third person to indicate an individual who has not been given his button, but who can be trusted nonetheless
Friend of ours	Used by a third person to indicate *un uomo combinato*, a 'made man'
Garbage business; waste management business	A polite euphemism for the Mafia's day-to-day business
Gift	A bribe, be it for a witness, a Fed or Sergeant O'Hoolihan

Give a pass	To let someone off from being iced
Going	About to be popped
Going south	Stealing; passing money under the table; going on the run.
Golden Age	The time before RICO made life more difficult
Goombah	An errand boy; someone who does things for you
Gregario	A bottom-rung member of the Family
Hard-on with a suitcase	A laywer in the pay of the Mafia
Half a hard-on with a suitcase	A female Mafia lawyer
Heavy	Packed, armed, as in: 'Come heavy' = make sure you're packing some serious lupara.
Infame	Infamous, treacherous
Jamook	Idiot, loser
Joint, the. Also: the can, the pen, go away to college, become a guest of the State.	Prison
Juice	Interest paid to a usurer; 'vig'
LCN	La Cosa Nostra – FBI terminology.
Lupara	A sawn-off shotgun, from the Italian lupo since such weapons were once used to hunt wolves. Now a catch-all term for Mafia weapons.
Made guy	An initiated member of the Family. Someone who has been 'straightened out' or who has 'got his button'
Make a marriage	To make an alliance of Families, so as to be able to deal with a particular problem
Mattresses, going to, taking it to, or hitting the	Going to war with a rival Family
Message job	Carefully shooting someone in a particular part of the body, to send a message to the victim's Family
The mob	A single organized crime Family OR all Families together
Moe Green Special	Shot through the eye, like Moe Green in The Godfather. See 'Message Job'
Mobbed up	Embroiled in Mafia business
Mustache Petes	Derogatory term for old-fashioned Mafiosi
Nut, the (il nocciolo)	'The bottom line'/the gross profit
Omertà	The Mafia's famous code of silence

Off the record	A deal or action not sanctioned by the Administration
Outfit	A crew, clan or Family within the Mafia
Padrino	Godfather
Pay tribute	Give the Boss a piece of the action, as a mark of respect
Pentito	A 'repentant'; someone who has chosen to squeal to the authorities in return for a commuted sentence
Pezzo da novanta	A Mafia leader
Picciotto	Literally in Italian 'a young man', but has come to mean any member of the lower echelons of the Family.
A piece	A gun
Pinched	Arrested
Pizzo	Protection money
Posato	Excommunicated from the mafia
Problem	A liability, someone likely to be taken for a short ride in the car
The program	The Feds' Witness Protection Program
Rat	A squealer, grass, snitch, *pentito*, canary
RICO	Racketeer Influenced and Corrupt Organizations Act. An American legal bill pushed through in 1970 that corresponded with a big clampdown on organized crime
Sbirro	Contemptuous Italian term for a policeman
Shake down	Blackmail; put the frighteners on someone
Shy	The interest charged on loans by money lenders
Soldier ('*soldato*')	The lowest members of the Family, who make up a 'crew'
Tax	To take a cut of someone's earnings
This thing of ours	*Cosa Nostra*; the Mafia.
Through the eye	A 'message job' through the eye to say 'we're watching you'. See 'Moe Green Special'.
Through the mouth	A 'message job' to indicate that someone was a *pentito*
Vig	Interest paid to a money lender, or the payment to a bookie for placing a bet
Wiseguy	A made man
Young Turks	Younger, wilder generation of Mafiosi, less likely to stick to the rules and live by the old traditions
Zio, Zi', Zu	Literally 'Uncle' – a term of respect for a Mafia godfather; synonym of 'Don'
Zips	Derogatory term for Sicilian Mafiosi, used by their American counterparts

Bibliography

Dickie, John, *Cosa Nostra*, Hodder and Stoughton, 2004.

Farrell, Joseph (ed), *Understanding The Mafia*, Manchester University Press, 1997.

Oliveri, Fabio, *La Gestualità dei Siciliani*, Krea, 2002.

Munari, Bruno, *Speak Italian: The Fine Art of the Gesture*, Chronicle, 2005.

Cangelosi, Don and Delli Carpini, Joseph, *Italian Without Words*, Meadowbrook Press, 1989.

Hughes, Lloyd, *The Rough Guide to Gangster Movies*, Rough Guides, 2005.

Thanks to Marco Gambino for his translations of some of the 'Useful clichés', and for his invaluable advice on the correct execution of all of the Italian gestures featured in this book.

Goodbye! (For ever)

Addio! (Per sempre)
[Ad-ee-OH! (Pear SEMpray)]